THIS HOLY BIBLE

Presented to

_____

_____

by _____

_____

Date _____

For the faithful in all English-speaking countries the publication of The New American Bible represents a notable achievement. Its pages contain a new Catholic version of the Bible in English, along with illustrations and explanations that facilitate the understanding of the text.

For more than a quarter of a century, members of the Catholic Biblical Association of America, sponsored by the Bishops' Committee of the Confraternity of Christian Doctrine, have labored to create this new translation of the Scriptures from the original languages or from the oldest extant form in which the texts exist.

In so doing, the translators have carried out the directive of our predecessor, Pius XII, in his famous Encyclical Divino Afflante Spiritu, and the decree of the Second Vatican Council (Dei Verbum), which prescribed that "up-to-date and appropriate translations be made in the various languages, by preference from the original texts of the sacred books," and that "with the approval of Church authority, these translations may be produced in cooperation with our separated brethren" so that "all Christians may be able to use them."

The holy task of spreading God's word to the widest possible readership has a special urgency today. Despite all his material achievements, man still struggles with the age-old problems of how to order his life for the glory of God, for the welfare of his fellows and the salvation of his soul. Therefore we are gratified to find in this new translation of the Scriptures a new opportunity for men to give themselves to frequent reading of, and meditation on, the living Word of God. In its pages we recognize His voice, we hear a message of deep significance for every one of us. Through the spiritual dynamism and prophetic force of the Bible, the Holy Spirit spreads his light and his warmth over all men, in whatever historical or sociological situation they find themselves.

On all who have contributed to this translation, and all who seek in its pages the sacred teaching and the promise of salvation of Jesus Christ our Lord, we gladly bestow our paternal Apostolic Blessing.

From the Vatican, September 18, 1970

Paulus P.P. VI-

THE NEW AMERICAN BIBLE

Translated from the Original Languages with Critical Use of All the Ancient Sources

AND

THE REVISED NEW TESTAMENT
AUTHORIZED BY THE BOARD OF TRUSTEES
OF THE
CONFRATERNITY OF CHRISTIAN DOCTRINE
AND
APPROVED BY THE ADMINISTRATIVE COMMITTEE/BOARD
OF THE
NATIONAL CONFERENCE OF CATHOLIC BISHOPS
AND THE
UNITED STATES CATHOLIC CONFERENCE

Our Sunday Visitor Publishing Division
Our Sunday Visitor, Inc.
Huntington, Indiana 46750

Old Testament

NIHIL OBSTAT: STEPHEN J. HARTDEGEN, O.F.M., L.L.S.
CHRISTIAN P. CEROKE, O. Carm., S.T.D.
IMPRIMATUR: ✠PATRICK CARDINAL O'BOYLE, D.D.
Archbishop of Washington
July 27, 1970

Revised Psalms
IMPRIMATUR: MOST REV. DANIEL E. PILARCZYK
President, National Conference of Catholic Bishops
October 10, 1991

Revised New Testament
NIHIL OBSTAT: STEPHEN J. HARTDEGEN, O.F.M., L.L.S.
Censor Deputatus
IMPRIMATUR: ✠JAMES A. HICKEY, S.T.D., J.C.D.
Archbishop of Washington
August 27, 1986

Reference Material
NIHIL OBSTAT: MICHAEL F. GUTGSELL, J.C.D.
VALENTINE J. PETER, S.T.D., J.C.D.
Censor Librorum
IMPRIMATUR: ✠DANIEL E. SHEEHAN, D.D., J.C.D.
Archbishop of Omaha
December 27, 1991

The Catholic Answer Inserts
NIHIL OBSTAT: GARY APPLEGATE, J.C.L.
Censor
IMPRIMATUR: ✠JAMES P. KELEHER, S.T.D.
Archbishop of Kansas City in Kansas
July 1, 2002

PREFACE

Throughout its existence, the Catholic Church has had its critics. They have challenged its witness, questioned its authority, even sought to use the very Scriptures it compiled to cast doubt upon its teachings. And for as long as there have been challenges, Catholics have responded by testifying to the truths upon which their Church was founded. Each generation has had to learn anew the Catholic answer.

Today, Catholics are still beset by critics. Some use the well-worn arguments of scriptural fundamentalism, while others use the language of modern science and philosophy. Catholics must be ready to answer both. In addition, today's Catholics, sometimes regardless of age, often do not have a full appreciation or understanding of why they believe what they believe. Many Catholics themselves are often searching for the Catholic answer.

In this Bible, the editors at Our Sunday Visitor, drawing on a long tradition of defining and defending the faith as publishers of *The Catholic Answer* magazine, join forces with Fireside Catholic Publishing, publishers of quality Catholic Bibles for three generations, in a unique partnership. For the first time, the eternal words of Scripture combine with concise and powerful answers to the questions every Catholic asks and will be asked about the faith. *The Catholic Answer Bible* is a dependable resource to help Catholics learn more about their faith so that they can better live its truth and defend its teachings. Herein lies the Catholic answer.

The Publishers

The Catholic Answer Bible

Published by
Fireside Catholic Publishing

In conjunction with
Our Sunday Visitor

© 2002

DeVore and Sons, Inc.
Wichita, Kansas USA

TABLE OF CONTENTS

The Catholic Answer Inserts

PAUL, BISHOP,
SERVANT OF THE SERVANTS OF GOD
TOGETHER WITH THE
FATHERS OF THE SACRED
COUNCIL

FOR EVERLASTING MEMORY

DOGMATIC
CONSTITUTION
ON DIVINE REVELATION

PREFACE

1. Hearing the Word of God with reverence and proclaiming it with faith, the sacred Synod takes its direction from these words of St. John: "We announce to you the eternal life which dwelt with the Father and was made visible to us. What we have seen and heard we announce to you, so that you may have fellowship with us and our common fellowship be with the Father and His Son Jesus Christ" (1 John 1; 2-3). Therefore, following in the footsteps of the Council of Trent and of the First Vatican Council, this present Council wishes to set forth authentic doctrine on divine revelation and how it is handed on, so that by hearing the message of salvation the whole world may believe, by believing it may hope, and by hoping it may love.[1]

CHAPTER 1

REVELATION ITSELF

2. In His goodness and wisdom God chose to reveal Himself and to make known to us the hidden purpose of His will (see Eph. 1: 9) by which through Christ, the Word made flesh, man might in the Holy Spirit have access to the Father and come to share in the divine nature (see Eph. 2: 18; 2 Peter 1: 4). Through this revelation, therefore, the invisible God (see Col. 1: 15; 1 Tim. 1: 17) out of the abundance of His love speaks to men as friends (see Ex. 33: 11; John 15: 14-15) and lives among them (see Bar. 3: 38), so that He may invite and take them into fellowship with Himself. This plan of revelation is realized by deeds and words having an inner unity: the deeds wrought by God in the history of salvation manifest and confirm the teaching and realities signified by the words, while the words proclaim the deeds and clarify the mystery contained in them. By this revelation then, the deepest truth about God and the salvation of man shines out for our sake in Christ, who is both the mediator and the fullness of all revelation.[2]

3. God, who through the Word creates all things (see John 1: 3) and keeps them in existence, gives men an enduring witness to Himself in created realities (see Rom. 1: 19-20). Planning to make known the way of heavenly salvation, He went further and from the start manifested Himself to our first parents. Then after their fall His promise of redemption aroused in them the hope of being saved (see Gen. 3: 15) and from that time on He ceaselessly kept the human race in His care, to give eternal life to those who perseveringly do good in search of salvation (see Rom. 2: 6-7). Then, at the time He had appointed He called Abraham in order to make of him a great nation (see Gen. 12:2). Through the patriarchs, and after them through Moses and the prophets, He taught this people to acknowledge Himself the one living and true God, provident father and just judge, and to wait for the Saviour promised by Him, and in this manner prepared the way for the Gospel down through the centuries.

4. Then, after speaking in many and varied ways through the prophets, "now at last in these days God has spoken to us in His Son" (Heb. 1: 1-2). For He sent His Son, the eternal Word, who enlightens all men, so that He might dwell among men and tell them of the innermost being of God (see John 1: 1-18). Jesus Christ, therefore, the Word made flesh, was sent as "a man to men."[3] He "speaks the words of God" (John 3: 34), and completes the work of salvation which His Father gave Him to do (see John 5: 36, 17: 4). To see Jesus is to see His Father (see John 14: 9). For this reason Jesus perfected revelation by fulfilling it through His whole work of making Himself present and manifesting Himself: through His

---

[1]Cf. St. Augustine, *De Catechizandis Rudibus*, C, IV, 8: PL. 40, 316.

[2]Cf. Mt. 11: 27; Jn. 1: 14 and 17; 14: 6; 17: 1-3; 2 Cor. 3: 16 and 4: 6; Eph. 1: 3-14.

[3]*Epistle to Diognetus*, c. VII, 4: Funk, *Apostolic Fathers*, I, p. 403.

words and deeds, His signs and wonders, but especially through His death and glorious resurrection from the dead and final sending of the Spirit of truth. Moreover He confirmed with divine testimony what revelation proclaimed, that God is with us to free us from the darkness of sin and death, and to raise us up to life eternal.

The Christian dispensation, therefore, as the new and definitive covenant, will never pass away and we now await no further new public revelation before the glorious manifestation of our Lord Jesus Christ (see 1 Tim. 6: 14 and Tit. 2: 13).

5. "The obedience of faith" (Rom. 16: 26; see Rom. 1: 5; 2 Cor. 10: 5-6) "is to be given to God who reveals, an obedience by which man commits his whole self freely to God, offering the full submission of intellect and will to God who reveals,"[4] and freely assenting to the truth revealed by Him. To make this act of faith, the grace of God and the interior help of the Holy Spirit must precede and assist, moving the heart and turning it to God, opening the eyes of the mind and giving "joy and ease to everyone in assenting to the truth and believing it."[5] To bring about an ever deeper understanding of revelation the same Holy Spirit constantly brings faith to completion by His gifts.

6. Through divine revelation, God chose to show forth and communicate Himself and the eternal decisions of His will regarding the salvation of men. That is to say, He chose to share with them those divine treasures which totally transcend the understanding of the human mind.[6]

As a sacred Synod has affirmed, God, the beginning and end of all things, can be known with certainty from created reality by light of human reason (see Rom. 1: 20); but it teaches that it is through His revelation "that those religious truths which are by their nature accessible to human reason can be known by all men with ease, with solid certitude and with no trace of error, even in this present state of the human race."[7]

CHAPTER II

HANDING ON DIVINE REVELATION

7. In His gracious goodness, God has seen to it that what He had revealed for the salvation of all nations would abide perpetually in its full integrity and be handed on to all generations. Therefore Christ the Lord in whom the full revelation of the supreme God is brought to completion (see 2 Cor. 1: 20; 3: 16; 4: 6), commissioned the Apostles to preach to all men that Gospel which is the source of all saving truth and moral teaching,[8] and to impart to them heavenly gifts. This Gospel had been promised in former times through the prophets, and Christ Himself had fulfilled it and promulgated it with His lips. This commission was faithfully fulfilled by the Apostles who, by their oral preaching, by example, and by observances handed on what they had received from the lips of Christ, from living with Him, and from what He did, or what they had learned through the prompting of the Holy Spirit. The commission was fulfilled, too, by those Apostles and apostolic men who under the inspiration of the same Holy Spirit committed the message of salvation to writing.[9]

But in order to keep the Gospel forever whole and alive within the Church, the Apostles left bishops as their successors, "handing over" to them "the authority to teach in their own place."[10] This sacred tradition, therefore, and Sacred Scripture of both the Old and New Testaments are like a mirror in which the pilgrim Church on earth looks at God, from whom she has received everything, until she is brought finally to see Him as He is, face to face (see 1 John 3: 2).

8. And so the apostolic preaching, which is expressed in a special way in the inspired books, was to be preserved by an unending succession of preachers until the end of time. Therefore the Apostles, handing on what they themselves had received, warn the faithful to hold fast to the traditions which they have learned either by word of mouth or by letter (see 2 Thess. 2: 15), and to fight in defense of the faith handed on once and for all (see Jud. 3).[11] Now what was handed on by the Apostles includes everything which contributes toward the holiness of life and increase in faith of the People of God; and so the Church, in her teaching, life and worship, perpetuates and hands on to all generations all that she herself is, all that she believes.

This tradition which comes from the Apostles develops in the Church with the help of

---

[4]First Vatican Council, *Dogmatic Constitution on the Catholic Faith*, Chap. 3, "On Faith:" Denzinger 1789 (3008).

[5]Second Council of Orange, Canon 7: Denzinger 180 (377); First Vatican Council, *loc. cit.*: Denzinger 1791 (3010).

[6]First Vatican Council, *Dogmatic Constitution on the Catholic Faith*, Chap. 2, "On Revelation:" Denzinger 1786 (3005).

[7]*Ibid*: Denzinger 1785 and 1786 (3004 and 3005).

[8]Cf. Matt. 28: 19-20, and Mark 16: 15; Council of Trent, session IV, *Decree on Scriptural Canons*: Denzinger 783 (1501).

[9]Cf. Council of Trent, *loc. cit.*; First Vatican Council, session III, *Dogmatic Constitution on the Catholic Faith*, Chap. 2, "On revelation:" Denzinger 1787 (3006).

[10]St. Irenaeus, *Against Heretics* III, 3, 1: PG 7, 848; Harvey, 2, p. 9.

[11]Cf. Second Council of Nicea: Denzinger 303 (602); Fourth Council of Constance, session X, Canon 1: Denzinger 336 (650-652).

the Holy Spirit.[12] For there is a growth in the understanding of the realities and the words which have been handed down. This happens through the contemplation and study made by believers, who treasure these things in their hearts (see Luke 2: 19, 51), through a penetrating understanding of the spiritual realities which they experience, and through the preaching of those who have received through episcopal succession the sure gift of truth. For as the centuries succeed one another, the Church constantly moves forward toward the fullness of divine truth until the words of God reach their complete fulfillment in her.

The words of the holy Fathers witness to the presence of this living tradition, whose wealth is poured into the practice and life of the believing and praying Church. Through the same tradition the Church's full canon of the sacred books is known, and the sacred writings themselves are more profoundly understood and unceasingly made active in her; and thus God, who spoke of old, uninterruptedly converses with the bride of His beloved Son; and the Holy Spirit, through whom the living voice of the Gospel resounds in the Church, and through her, in the world, leads unto all truth those who believe and makes the Word of Christ dwell abundantly in them (see Col. 3: 16).

9. Hence there exists a close connection and communication between sacred tradition and sacred Scripture. For both of them, flowing from the same divine wellspring, in a certain way merge into a unity and tend toward the same end. For sacred Scripture is the Word of God inasmuch as it is consigned to writing under the inspiration of the divine Spirit, while sacred tradition takes the Word of God entrusted by Christ the Lord and the Holy Spirit to the Apostles, and hands it on to their successors in its full purity, so that led by the light of the Spirit of truth, they may in proclaiming it preserve this Word of God faithfully, explain it, and make it more widely known. Consequently it is not from sacred Scripture alone that the Church draws her certainty about everything which has been revealed. Therefore both sacred tradition and sacred Scripture are to be accepted and venerated with the same sense of loyalty and reverence.[13]

10. Sacred tradition and sacred Scripture form one sacred deposit of the Word of God, committed to the Church. Holding fast to this deposit the entire holy people united with their shepherds remain always steadfast in the teaching of the Apostles, in the common life, in the breaking of the bread and in prayers (see

Acts 8: 42, Greek text), so that holding to, practicing and professing the heritage of the faith, it becomes on the part of the bishops and faithful a single common effort.[14]

But the task of authentically interpreting the Word of God, whether written or handed on,[15] has been entrusted exclusively to the living teaching office of the Church,[16] whose authority is exercised in the name of Jesus Christ. This teaching office is not above the Word of God, but serves it, teaching only what has been handed on, listening to it devoutly, guarding it scrupulously and explaining it faithfully in accord with a divine commission and with the help of the Holy Spirit; it draws from this one deposit of faith everything which it presents for belief as divinely revealed.

It is clear, therefore, that sacred tradition, sacred Scripture and the teaching authority of the Church, in accord with God's most wise design, are so linked and joined together that one cannot stand without the others, and that all together and each in its own way under the action of the one Holy Spirit contribute effectively to the salvation of souls.

CHAPTER III

SACRED SCRIPTURE, ITS INSPIRATION AND DIVINE INTERPRETATION

11. Those divinely revealed realities which are contained and presented in sacred Scripture have been committed to writing under the inspiration of the Holy Spirit. For holy mother Church, relying on the belief of the Apostles (see John 20: 31; 2 Tim. 3: 16; 2 Peter 1: 19-21; 3: 15-16), holds that the books of both the Old and New Testaments in their entirety, with all their parts, are sacred and canonical because written under the inspiration of the Holy Spirit, they have God as their author and have been handed on as such to the Church herself.[17] In composing the sacred books, God chose men and while employed by Him[18] they made use of their powers and abil-

---

[12]Cf. First Vatican Council, *Dogmatic Constitution on the Catholic Faith*, Chap. 4, "On Faith and Reason:" Denzinger 1800 (3020).

[13]Cf. Council of Trent, session IV, *loc. cit.*: Denzinger 783 (1501).

[14]Cf. Pius XII, apostolic constitution, *Munificentissimus Deus*, Nov. 1, 1950: AAS 42 (1950) p. 756; Collected Writings of St. Cyprian, Letter 66, 8: Hartel, III B, p. 733: "The Church [is] people united with the priest and the pastor together with his flock."

[15]Cf. First Vatican Council, *Dogmatic Constitution on the Catholic Faith*, Chap. 3 "On Faith:" Denzinger 1792 (3011).

[16]Cf. Pius XII, Encyclical Letter *Humani Generis*, Aug. 12, 1950: AAS 42 (1950) pp. 568-69: Denzinger 2314 (3886).

[17]Cf. First Vatican Council, *Dogmatic Constitution on the Catholic Faith*, Chap. 2 "On Revelation:" Denzinger 1787 (3006); Biblical Commission, Decree of June 18, 1915: Denzinger 2180 (3629): EB 420; Holy Office, Epistle of Dec. 22, 1923: EB 499.

[18]Cf. Pius XII, Encyclical Letter *Divino Afflante Spiritu*, Sept. 30, 1943: AAS 35 (1943) p. 314; Enchiridion Biblic. (EB) 556.

ities, so that with Him acting in them and through them,[19] they, as true authors, consigned to writing everything and only those things which He wanted.[20]

Therefore since everything asserted by the inspired authors or sacred writers must be held to be asserted by the Holy Spirit, it follows that the books of Scripture must be acknowledged as teaching solidly, faithfully and without error that truth which God wanted put into the sacred writings[21] for the sake of our salvation. Therefore "all Scripture is divinely inspired and has its use for teaching the truth and refuting error, for reformation of manners and discipline in right living, so that the man who belongs to God may be efficient and equipped for good work of every kind" (2 Tim. 3: 16-17, Greek text).

12. However, since God speaks in sacred Scripture through men in human fashion,[22] the interpreter of sacred Scripture, in order to see clearly what God wanted to communicate to us, should carefully investigate what meaning the sacred writers really intended, and what God wanted to manifest by means of their words.

To search out the intention of the sacred writers, attention should be given, among other things, to "literary forms." For truth is set forth and expressed differently in texts which are variously historical, prophetic, poetic, or of other forms of discourse. The interpreter must investigate what meaning the sacred writer intended to express and actually expressed in particular circumstances by using contemporary literary forms in accordance with the situation of his own time and culture.[23] For the correct understanding of what the sacred author wanted to assert, due attention must be paid to the customary and characteristic styles of feeling, speaking and narrating which prevailed at the time of the sacred writer, and to the patterns men normally employed at that period in their everyday dealings with one another.[24]

But, since holy Scripture must be read and interpreted in the same spirit in which it was written,[25] no less serious attention must be given to the content and unity of the whole of Scripture if the meaning of the sacred texts is to be correctly worked out. The living tradition of the whole Church must be taken into account along with the harmony which exists between elements of the faith. It is the task of exegetes to work according to these rules toward a better understanding and explanation of the meaning of sacred Scripture, so that through preparatory study the judgment of the Church may mature. For all of what has been said about the way of interpreting Scripture is subject finally to the judgment of the Church, which carries out the divine commission and ministry of guarding and interpreting the Word of God.[26]

13. In sacred Scripture, therefore while the truth and holiness of God always remains intact, the marvelous "condescension" of eternal wisdom is clearly shown, "that we may learn the gentle kindness of God, which words cannot express, and how far He has gone in adapting His language with thoughtful concern for our weak human nature."[27] For the words of God, expressed in human language, have been made like human discourse, just as the word of the eternal Father, when He took to Himself the flesh of human weakness, was in every way made like men.

CHAPTER IV

THE OLD TESTAMENT

14. In carefully planning and preparing the salvation of the whole human race the God of infinite love, by a special dispensation, chose for Himself a people to whom He would entrust His promises. First He entered into a covenant with Abraham (see Gen. 15: 18) and, through Moses, with the people of Israel (see Ex. 24: 8). To this people which He had acquired for Himself, He so manifested Himself through words and deeds as the one true and living God that Israel came to know by experience the ways of God with men. Then, too, when God Himself spoke to them through the mouth of the prophets, Israel daily gained a deeper and clearer understanding of His ways and made them more widely known among the nations (see Ps. 21: 29; 95: 1-3; Is. 2: 1-4; Jer. 3: 17). The plan of salvation foretold by the sacred authors, recounted and explained by them, is found as the true Word of God in the

---

[19]"In" and "for" man: cf. Heb. 1: 1 and 4: 7; ("in"): 2 Sm. 23: 2; Mt. 1: 22 and various places; ("for"): First Vatican Council, *Schema on Catholic Doctrine*, note 9: Coll. Lac. VII, 522.

[20]Leo XIII, Encyclical Letter *Providentissimus Deus*, Nov. 18, 1893: Denzinger 1952 (3293); EB 125.

[21]Cf. St. Augustine, *Gen. ad Litt.* 2, 9, 20: PL 34, 270-271; Epistle 82, 3: PL 33, 277: CSEL 34, 2, p. 354.
–St. Thomas, "On Truth," Q. 12, A. 2, C.
–Council of Trent, session IV, *Scriptural Canons:* Denzinger 783 (1501).
Leo XIII, Encyclical Letter *Providentissimus Deus:* EB 121, 124, 126-127.
–Pius XII, Encyclical Letter *Divino Afflante Spiritu:* EB 539.

[22]St. Augustine, *City of God,* XVII, 6, 2: PL 537: CSEL XL, 2, 228.

[23]St. Augustine, *On Christian Doctrine* III, 18, 26; PL 34, 75-76.

[24]Pius XII, *Loc. cit.:* Denzinger 2294 (3829-3830); EB 557-562.

[25]Cf. Benedict XV, Encyclical Letter *Spiritus Paraclitus,* Sept. 15, 1920: EB 469. St. Jerome, "In Galatians" 5, 19-20: PL 26, 417 A.

[26]Cf. First Vatican Council, *Dogmatic Constitution on the Catholic Faith,* Chapter 2, "On Revelation:" Denzinger 1788 (3007).

[27]St. John Chrysostom *In Genesis* 3, 8 (Homily 17, 1): PG 53, 134; "Attemperatio" [in English "Suitable adjustment"] in Greek "synkatabasis."

books of the Old Testament: these books, therefore, written under divine inspiration, remain permanently valuable. "For all that was written for our instruction, so that by steadfastness and the encouragement of the Scriptures we might have hope" (Rom. 15: 4).

15. The principal purpose to which the plan of the old covenant was directed was to prepare for the coming of Christ, the redeemer of all and of the messianic kingdom, to announce this coming by prophecy (see Luke 24: 44; John 5: 39; 1 Peter 1: 10), and to indicate its meaning through various types (see 1 Cor. 10: 11). Now the books of the Old Testament, in accordance with the state of mankind before the time of salvation established by Christ, reveal to all men the knowledge of God and of man and the ways in which God, just and merciful, deals with men. These books, though they also contain some things which are incomplete and temporary, nevertheless show us true divine pedagogy.[28] These same books, then, give expression to a lively sense of God, contain a store of sublime teachings about God, sound wisdom about human life, and a wonderful treasury of prayers, and in them the mystery of our salvation is present in a hidden way. Christians should receive them with reverence.

16. God, the inspirer and author of both Testaments, wisely arranged that the New Testament be hidden in the Old and the Old be made manifest in the New.[29] For, though Christ established the new covenant in His blood (see Luke 22: 20; 1 Cor. 11: 25), still the books of the Old Testament with all their parts, caught up into the proclamation of the Gospel,[30] acquire and show forth their full meaning in the New Testament (see Matt. 5: 17; Luke 24: 27; Rom. 16: 25-26; 2 Cor. 3: 14-16) and in turn shed light on it and explain it.

CHAPTER V

THE NEW TESTAMENT

17. The Word of God, which is the power of God for the salvation of all who believe (see Rom. 1: 16), is set forth and shows its power in a most excellent way in the writings of the New Testament. For when the fullness of time arrived (see Gal. 4: 4), the Word was made flesh and dwelt among us in His fullness of graces and truth (see John 1: 14). Christ established the Kingdom of God on earth, manifested His Father and Himself by deeds and

words, and completed His work by His death, resurrection and glorious ascension and by the sending of the Holy Spirit. Having been lifted up from the earth, He draws all men to Himself (see John 12: 32, Greek text), He who alone has the words of eternal life (see John 6: 68). This mystery had not been manifested to other generations as it was now revealed to His holy Apostles and prophets in the Holy Spirit (see Eph. 3: 4-6, Greek text), so that they might preach the Gospel, stir up faith in Jesus, Christ and Lord, and gather together the Church. Now the writings of the New Testament stand as a perpetual and divine witness to these realities.

18. It is common knowledge that among all the Scriptures, even those of the New Testament, the Gospels have a special preeminence, and rightly so, for they are the principal witness for the life and teaching of the Incarnate Word, our Savior.

The Church has always and everywhere held and continues to hold that the four Gospels are of apostolic origin. For what the Apostles preached in fulfillment of the commission of Christ, afterwards they themselves and apostolic men, under the inspiration of the divine Spirit, handed on to us in writing: the foundation of faith, namely, the fourfold Gospel, according to Matthew, Mark, Luke and John.[31]

19. Holy Mother Church has firmly and with absolute constancy held, and continues to hold, that the four Gospels just named, whose historical character the Church unhesitatingly asserts, faithfully hand on what Jesus Christ, while living among men, really did and taught for their eternal salvation until the day He was taken up into heaven (see Acts 1: 1-2). Indeed, after the ascension of the Lord the Apostles handed on to their hearers what He had said and done. This they did with that clearer understanding which they enjoyed[32] after they had been instructed by the glorious events of Christ's life and taught by the light of the Spirit of truth.[33] The sacred authors wrote the four Gospels, selecting some things from the many which had been handed on by word of mouth or in writing, reducing some of them to a synthesis, explaining some things in view of the situation of their churches, and preserving the form of proclamation but always in such fashion that they told us the honest truth about Jesus.[34] For their intention in writing was that either from their own memory and recollections, or from the witness of those who "themselves from the beginning were eyewit-

[28]Pius XI Encyclical Epistle *Mit Brennender Sorge*, March 14, 1937: AAS 29 (1937) p. 51.

[29]St. Augustine, *Quest in Hept.* 2, 73: PL 34, 623.

[30]St. Irenaeus, *Against Heretics* III, 21, 3: PG 7, 950; (Same as 25, 1: Harvey 2, p. 115). St. Cyril of Jerusalem, *Catech.* 4, 35; PG 33, 497. Theodore of Mopsuestia, *In Soph.* 1, 4-6: PG 66, 452D-453A.

[31]Cf. St. Irenaeus, *Against Heretics* III, 11, 8: PG 7, 885; Sagnard Edition, p. 194.

[32]John 2: 22; 12: 16; Cf. 14: 26; 16: 12-13; 7: 39.

[33]Cf. John 14: 26; 16: 13.

[34]Cf. instruction *Holy Mother Church* edited by Pontifical Consilium for Promotion of Bible Studies: AAS 56 (1964) p. 715.

nesses and ministers of the Word" we might know "the truth" concerning those matters about which we have been instructed (see Luke 1: 2-4).

20. Besides the four Gospels, the canon of the New Testament also contains the epistles of St. Paul and other apostolic writings, composed under the inspiration of the Holy Spirit, by which according to the wise plan of God, those matters which concern Christ the Lord are confirmed, His true teaching is more and more fully stated, the saving power of the divine work of Christ is preached, the story is told of the beginnings of the Church and its marvelous growth, and its glorious fulfillment is foretold.

For the Lord Jesus was with His Apostles as He had promised (see Matt. 28: 20) and sent them the advocate Spirit who would lead them into the fullness of truth (see John 16: 13).

CHAPTER VI

SACRED SCRIPTURE IN THE LIFE OF THE CHURCH

21. The Church has always venerated the divine Scriptures just as she venerates the body of the Lord, since, especially in the sacred liturgy, she unceasingly receives and offers to the faithful the bread of life from the table both of God's Word and of Christ's Body. She has always maintained them, and continues to do so, together with sacred tradition, as the supreme rule of faith, since, as inspired by God and committed once and for all to writing, they impart the Word of God Himself without change, and make the voice of the Holy Spirit resound in the words of the prophets and Apostles. Therefore, like the Christian religion itself, all the preaching of the Church must be nourished and regulated by sacred Scripture. For in the sacred books, the Father who is in heaven meets His children with great love and speaks with them; and the force and power in the word of God is so great that it stands as the support and energy of the Church, the strength of faith for her sons, the food of the soul, the pure and everlasting source of spiritual life. Consequently these words are perfectly applicable to sacred Scripture: "For the word of God is living and active" (Heb. 4: 12) and "it has power to build you up and give you your heritage among all those who are sanctified" (Acts 20: 32; see 1 Thess. 2: 13).

22. Easy access to sacred Scripture should be provided for all the Christian faithful. That is why the Church from the very beginning accepted as her own that very ancient Greek translation of the Old Testament which is called the septuagint; and she has always given a place of honor to other Eastern translations

and Latin ones, especially the Latin translation known as the vulgate. But since the Word of God should be accessible at all times, the Church by her authority and with maternal concern sees to it that suitable and correct translations are made into different languages, especially from the original texts of the sacred books. And should the opportunity arise and the Church authorities approve, if these translations are produced in cooperation with the separated brethren as well, all Christians will be able to use them.

23. The bride of the Incarnate Word, the Church taught by the Holy Spirit, is concerned to move ahead toward a deeper understanding of the sacred Scriptures so that she may increasingly feed her sons with the divine words. Therefore, she also encourages the study of the holy Fathers of both East and West and of sacred liturgies. Catholic exegetes then and other students of sacred theology, working diligently together and using appropriate means, should devote their energies, under the watchful care of the sacred teaching office of the Church, to an exploration and exposition of the divine writings. This should be so done that as many ministers of the divine word as possible will be able effectively to provide the nourishment of the Scriptures for the People of God, to enlighten their minds, strengthen their wills, and set men's hearts on fire with the love of God.[35] The sacred Synod encourages the sons of the Church and Biblical scholars to continue energetically, following the mind of the Church, with the work they have so well begun, with a constant renewal of vigor.[36]

24. Sacred theology rests on the written Word of God, together with sacred tradition, as its primary and perpetual foundation. By scrutinizing in the light of faith all truth stored up in the mystery of Christ, theology is most powerfully strengthened and constantly rejuvenated by that Word. For the sacred Scriptures contain the Word of God and since they are inspired really are the Word of God; and so the study of the sacred page is, as it were, the soul of sacred theology.[37] By the same word of Scripture the ministry of the Word also, that is, pastoral preaching, catechetics and all Christian instruction, in which the liturgical homily must hold the foremost place, is nourished in a healthy way and flourishes in a holy way.

25. Therefore, all the clergy must hold fast to the sacred Scriptures through diligent

[35]Cf. Pius XII, Encyclical Letter *Divino Afflante Spiritu:* EB 551, 553, 567.
—Pontifical Biblical Commission, *Instruction on Proper Teaching of Sacred Scripture in Seminaries and Religious Colleges,* May 13, 1950: AAS 42 (1950) pp. 495-505.
[36]Cf. Pius XII, *ibid:* EB 569.
[37]Cf. Leo XIII, Encyclical Letter *Providentissimus Deus:* EB 114; Benedict XV, Encyclical Letter *Spiritus paraclitus:* EB 483.

sacred reading and careful study, especially the priests of Christ and others, such as deacons and catechists who are legitimately active in the ministry of the Word. This is to be done so that none of them will become "an empty preacher of the word of God outwardly, who is not a listener to it inwardly"[38] since they must share the abundant wealth of the divine Word with the faithful committed to them, especially in the sacred liturgy. The sacred Synod also earnestly and especially urges all the Christian faithful, especially Religious, to learn by frequent reading of the divine Scriptures the "excellent knowledge of Jesus Christ" (Phil. 3: 8). "For ignorance of the Scriptures is ignorance of Christ."[39] Therefore, they should gladly put themselves in touch with the sacred text itself, whether it be through the liturgy, rich in the divine Word or through devotional reading, or through instructions suitable for the purpose and other aids which, in our time, with approval and active support of the shepherds of the Church, are commendably spread everywhere. And let them remember that prayer should accompany the reading of the sacred Scripture, so that God and man may talk together; for "we speak to Him when we pray; we hear Him when we read the divine saying."[40]

It devolves on sacred bishops "who have the apostolic teaching"[41] to give the faithful entrusted to them suitable instruction in the right use of the divine books, especially the New Testament and above all the Gospels.

This can be done through translations of the sacred texts, which are to be provided with the necessary and really adequate explanations so that the children of the Church may safely and profitably become conversant with the sacred Scriptures and be penetrated with their spirit.

Furthermore, editions of the sacred Scriptures, provided with suitable footnotes, should be prepared also for the use of non-Christians and adapted to their situation. Both pastors of souls and Christians generally should see to the wise distribution of these in one way or another.

26. In this way, therefore, through the reading and study of the sacred books "the word of God may spread rapidly and be glorified" (2 Thess. 3: 1) and the treasure of revelation, entrusted to the Church, may more and more fill the hearts of men. Just as the life of the Church is strengthened through more frequent celebration of the Eucharistic mystery, similarly we may hope for a new stimulus for the life of the Spirit from a growing reverence for the word of God, which "lasts forever" (Is. 40: 8, see 1 Peter 1: 23-25).

‡ ‡ ‡ ‡

The entire text and all the individual elements which have been set forth in this Constitution have pleased the Fathers. And by the Apostolic power conferred on us by Christ, we, together with the Venerable Fathers, in the Holy Spirit, approve, decree and enact them; and we order that what has been thus enacted in Council be promulgated, to the glory of God.

Rome, at St. Peter's 18 November, 1965

I, PAUL, Bishop of the Catholic Church

There follow the signatures of the Fathers.

---

[38]St. Augustine, Sermons, 179, 1: PL 38, 966.

[39]St. Jerome, Commentary on Isaiah, Prol: PL 24, 17.

Cf. Benedict XV, Encyclical Letter Spiritus paraclitus: EB 475-480; Pius XII, Encyclical Letter Divino Afflante Spiritu: EB 544.

[40]St. Ambrose, On the Duties of Ministers I, 20, 88: PL 16, 50.

[41]St. Irenaeus, Against Heretics IV, 32, 1: PG 7, 1071; (Same as 49, 2) Harvey, 2, p. 255.

Translation of the Second Vatican Council's "Dogmatic Constitution on Divine Revelation" reprinted by permission of the Publications Office, United States Catholic Conference, Washington, D.C.

THE BOOKS OF THE BIBLE

THE OLD TESTAMENT

THE NEW TESTAMENT

THE BOOKS OF THE OLD AND NEW TESTAMENTS AND THEIR ABBREVIATIONS

THE OLD TESTAMENT

Book	Abbrev.	Page	Book	Abbrev.	Page
Genesis	Gn	6	Proverbs	Prv	634
Exodus	Ex	58	Ecclesiastes	Eccl	664
Leviticus	Lv	95	Song of Songs	Sg	673
Numbers	Nm	122	Wisdom	Wis	680
Deuteronomy	Dt	161	Sirach	Sir	699
Joshua	Jos	195	Isaiah	Is	746
Judges	Jgs	217	Jeremiah	Jer	803
Ruth	Ru	238	Lamentations	Lam	859
1 Samuel	1 Sm	243	Baruch	Bar	866
2 Samuel	2 Sm	272	Ezekiel	Ez	874
1 Kings	1 Kgs	295	Daniel	Dn	917
2 Kings	2 Kgs	321	Hosea	Hos	936
1 Chronicles	1 Chr	347	Joel	Jl	947
2 Chronicles	2 Chr	374	Amos	Am	951
Ezra	Ezr	404	Obadiah	Ob	959
Nehemiah	Neh	414	Jonah	Jon	961
Tobit	Tb	428	Micah	Mi	964
Judith	Jdt	442	Nahum	Na	970
Esther	Est	456	Habakkuk	Hb	973
1 Maccabees	1 Mc	468	Zephaniah	Zep	976
2 Maccabees	2 Mc	497	Haggai	Hg	979
Job	Jb	519	Zechariah	Zec	982
Psalms	Ps(s)	547	Malachi	Mal	991

THE NEW TESTAMENT

Book	Abbrev.	Page	Book	Abbrev.	Page
Matthew	Mt	1005	1 Timothy	1 Tm	1306
Mark	Mk	1063	2 Timothy	2 Tm	1313
Luke	Lk	1090	Titus	Ti	1318
John	Jn	1135	Philemon	Phlm	1321
Acts of the Apostles	Acts	1169	Hebrews	Heb	1323
Romans	Rom	1208	James	Jas	1341
1 Corinthians	1 Cor	1229	1 Peter	1 Pt	1347
2 Corinthians	2 Cor	1251	2 Peter	2 Pt	1354
Galatians	Gal	1268	1 John	1 Jn	1359
Ephesians	Eph	1277	2 John	2 Jn	1365
Philippians	Phil	1285	3 John	3 Jn	1367
Colossians	Col	1292	Jude	Jude	1369
1 Thessalonians	1 Thes	1298	Revelation	Rv	1372
2 Thessalonians	2 Thes	1302			

The Names and Order of All the

BOOKS OF THE OLD AND NEW TESTAMENTS

Alphabetically Arranged

Book	Abbrev.		Page	Book	Abbrev.		Page
Acts of the Apostles	Acts	NT†	1169	2 Kings	2 Kgs	OT	321
Amos	Am	OT*	951	Lamentations	Lam	OT	859
Baruch	Bar	OT	866	Leviticus	Lv	OT	95
1 Chronicles	1 Chr	OT	347	Luke	Lk	NT	1090
2 Chronicles	2 Chr	OT	374	1 Maccabees	1 Mc	OT	468
Colossians	Col	NT	1292	2 Maccabees	2 Mc	OT	497
1 Corinthians	1 Cor	NT	1229	Malachi	Mal	OT	991
2 Corinthians	2 Cor	NT	1251	Mark	Mk	NT	1063
Daniel	Dn	OT	917	Matthew	Mt	NT	1005
Deuteronomy	Dt	OT	161	Micah	Mi	OT	964
Ecclesiastes	Eccl	OT	664	Nahum	Na	OT	970
Ephesians	Eph	NT	1277	Nehemiah	Neh	OT	414
Esther	Est	OT	456	Numbers	Nm	OT	122
Exodus	Ex	OT	58	Obadiah	Ob	OT	959
Ezekiel	Ez	OT	874	1 Peter	1 Pt	NT	1347
Ezra	Ezr	OT	404	2 Peter	2 Pt	NT	1354
Galatians	Gal	NT	1268	Philemon	Phlm	NT	1321
Genesis	Gn	OT	6	Philippians	Phil	NT	1285
Habakkuk	Hb	OT	973	Proverbs	Prv	OT	634
Haggai	Hg	OT	979	Psalms	Ps(s)	OT	547
Hebrews	Heb	NT	1323	Revelation	Rv	NT	1372
Hosea	Hos	OT	936	Romans	Rom	NT	1208
Isaiah	Is	OT	746	Ruth	Ru	OT	238
James	Jas	NT	1341	1 Samuel	1 Sm	OT	243
Jeremiah	Jer	OT	803	2 Samuel	2 Sm	OT	272
Job	Jb	OT	519	Sirach	Sir	OT	699
Joel	Jl	OT	947	Song of Songs	Sg	OT	673
John	Jn	NT	1135	1 Thessalonians	1 Thes	NT	1298
1 John	1 Jn	NT	1359	2 Thessalonians	2 Thes	NT	1302
2 John	2 Jn	NT	1365	1 Timothy	1 Tm	NT	1306
3 John	3 Jn	NT	1367	2 Timothy	2 Tm	NT	1313
Jonah	Jon	OT	961	Titus	Ti	NT	1318
Joshua	Jos	OT	195	Tobit	Tb	OT	428
Jude	Jude	NT	1369	Wisdom	Wis	OT	680
Judges	Jgs	OT	217	Zechariah	Zec	OT	982
Judith	Jdt	OT	442	Zephaniah	Zep	OT	976
1 Kings	1 Kgs	OT	295				

* OT—Old Testament   † NT—New Testament

COLLABORATORS ON THE OLD TESTAMENT THE NEW AMERICAN BIBLE

Bishops' Committee
The Confraternity of Christian Doctrine

Most Rev. Charles P. Greco, D.D., Chairman

Most Rev. Joseph T. McGucken, S.T.D.
Most Rev. Vincent S. Waters, D.D.

Most Rev. Romeo Blanchette, D.D.
Most Rev. Christopher J. Weldon, D.D.

Editors in Chief

Rev. Louis F. Hartman, C.SS.R., S.S.L., Ling. Or. L., Chairman
Rev. Msgr. Patrick W. Skehan, S.T.D., LL.D., Vice Chairman
Rev. Stephen J. Hartdegen, O.F.M., S.S.L., Secretary

Associate Editors and Translators

Rev. Edward P. Arbez, S.S., S.T.D.
Rev. Msgr. Edward J. Byrne, Ph.D., S.T.D.
Rev. Edward A. Cerny, S.S., S.T.D.
Rev. James E. Coleran, S.J., S.T.L., S.S.L.
Rev. John J. Collins, S.J., M.A., S.S.L.
Sr. M. Emmanuel Collins, O.S.F., Ph.D.
Prof. Frank M. Cross, Jr., Ph.D.
Rev. Patrick Cummins, O.S.B., S.T.D.
Rev. Antonine A. De Guglielmo, O.F.M., S.T.D., S.S.L., S.S. Lect. Gen.
Rev. Alexander A. Di Lella, O.F.M., S.T.L., S.S.L., Ph.D.
Most Rev. John J. Dougherty, S.T.L., S.S.D.
Rev. William A. Dowd, S.J., S.T.D., S.S.L.
Prof. David Noel Freedman, Ph.D.
Rev. Michael J. Gruenthaner, S.J., S.T.D., S.S.D.
Rev. Msgr. Maurice A. Hofer, S.S.L.
Rev. Justin Krellner, O.S.B., S.T.D.
Rev. Jospeh L. Lilly, C.M., S.T.D., S.S.L.
Rev. Roderick F. MacKenzie, S.J., M.A., S.S.D.
Rev. Edward A. Mangan, C.SS.R., S.S.L.

Rev. Daniel W. Martin, C.M., S.T.L., S.S.L.
Rev. William H. McClellan, S.J.
Rev. James McGlinchey, C.M., S.T.D.
Rev. Frederick Moriarty, S.J., S.S.L., S.T.D.
Rev. Richard T. Murphy, O.P., S.T.D., S.S.D.
Rev. Roland E. Murphy, O. Carm., M.A., S.T.D., S.S.L.
Rev. Msgr. William R. Newton, M.S., S.S.D.
Rev. Eberhard Olinger, O.S.B.
Rev. Charles H. Pickar, O.S.A., S.T.L., S.S.L.
Rev. Christopher Rehwinkel, O.F.M., S.T.D., S.S. Lect. Gen.
Rev. Msgr. John R. Rowan, S.T.D., S.S.L.
Prof. J.A. Sanders, Ph.D.
Rev. Edward F. Siegman, C.PP.S., S.T.D., S.S.L.
Rev. Msgr. Matthew P. Stapleton, S.T.D., S.S.L.
Rev. Msgr. John E. Steinmueller, S.T.D., S.S.L.
Rev. John Ujlaki, O.S.B., Litt. D.
Rev. Bruce Vawter, C.M., S.T.L., S.S.D.
Rev. John B. Weisengoff, S.T.D., S.S.L.

COLLABORATORS ON THE REVISED EDITION
THE NEW TESTAMENT
THE NEW AMERICAN BIBLE

Bishops' Ad Hoc Committee

Most Rev. Theodore E. McCarrick, D.D.
Most Rev. Richard J. Sklba, D.D.
Most Rev. J. Francis Stafford, D.D.
Most Rev. John F. Whealon, D.D., Chairman

Board of Editors

Rev. Msgr. Myles M. Bourke
Rev. Francis T. Gignac, S.J., Chairman
Rev. Stephen J. Hartdegen, O.F.M., Secretary
Rev. Claude J. Peifer, O.S.B.
Rev. John H. Reumann

Revisers

Rev. Msgr. Myles M. Bourke
Rev. Frederick W. Danker
Rev. Alexander A. Di Lella, O.F.M.
Rev. Charles H. Giblin, S.J.
Rev. Francis T. Gignac, S.J.
Rev. Stephen J. Hartdegen, O.F.M.
Dr. Maurya P. Horgan

Rev. John R. Keating, S.J.
Rev. John Knox
Dr. Paul J. Kobelski
Dr. J. Rebecca Lyman
Bro. Elliott C. Maloney, O.S.B.
Dr. Janet A. Timbie

Consultants

Rev. Joseph Jensen, O.S.B.
Rev. Aidan Kavanagh, O.S.B.
Dr. Marianne Sawicki

Business Manager

Charles A. Buggé

Word Processor

Suzanna Jordan

ORIGIN, INSPIRATION, AND HISTORY OF THE BIBLE

ORIGIN OF THE BIBLE

NO BOOK in the history of the world has wielded as much influence on civilization as the Holy Bible. The Bible is unique in that it had God as its Author, while all other books were composed by human beings. It is indeed, the Book of Books.

THE DEPOSIT OF FAITH

The Catholic Church derives all of its teaching authority from its tradition, the doctrine which has come down to it from Christ. This tradition is preserved in written form in the "Bible" which contains the principle truths of faith taught to the Apostles by Christ.

Inspired men were moved by the Spirit of God to commit these matters to writing in the early church. Only a short time after Christ's Ascension, perhaps within twenty years, the need to preserve these truths in a permanent form was recognized. Before any book was accepted as "authentic" however, the authority of an Apostle was demanded by the early Christian communities. Mark's Gospel was accepted because he was Peter's companion. Similarly, though Luke was a man who had not seen Christ, his book gained acceptance through St. Paul's authority.

The Church has protected and guarded these books which contained the revelations of Christ to His disciples and their testimony concerning Him.

THE BIBLE DEFINED

The other source of supernatural knowledge is the Bible. In the words of the Council of Trent, which enumerated the books of the Bible under their proper titles, the Church declares that she receives: "All the books of the Testaments, Old and New, since the one God is the Author of both." The Vatican Council is more explicit: "The Church holds those books as sacred and canonical, not because, having been composed by human industry, they were afterwards approved by her authority, nor merely because they contain revelation without error, but because having been written under the inspiration of the Holy Spirit, they have God as their Author.''

The word ''Bible'' comes from the Greek *biblion* meaning ''the book;'' the plural is *ta biblia*, ''the books.'' In the Greek the word is a neuter, but later on the word *biblia* was taken for a feminine singular, ''the book.'' Taken in this sense, it refers to all the books of both Testaments. The Bible is the Book par excellence.

THE BIBLE NEEDS AN INTERPRETER

The Bible is extremely difficult to understand, even by Bible scholars. It was written in languages long dead, and in the manner and idiom of the time. To interpret the Bible, it is not only necessary to understand the languages in which the Bible was written, but to understand the meanings that the words of the Bible had at the time they were written. The Bible, therefore, has to be interpreted to be understood, and for Catholics, the Church, guided by the Holy Spirit, is the official guardian and infallible interpreter of the Bible.

CANON OF THE BIBLE

The Bible contains 72 books (or 73, depending on whether the Book of Lamentations is listed as a separate book and not as a part of Jeremiah), varying in length from a few hundred words to many thousands. Together, these books comprise the official list or canon of the Bible. Of these books, 45 were written before the time of Christ and are called the books of the Old Testament. The other 27 books were written after the time of Christ and are called the books of the New Testament.

MEANING OF THE WORD ''TESTAMENT''

The meaning of the word ''testament'' as used here is that of a pact, an agreement, or a covenant. The Old Testament is the pact or alliance that God made first with the Patriarchs and then with the Jewish people through Moses; a Saviour is promised and a Law is proclaimed, and salvation is through the Law.

The New Testament is the covenant or the alliance that God made with all men whereby, through the mediatorship of His Son, Jesus Christ, all men can be saved.

DETERMINATION OF THE BIBLE CANON

At the time the books of the New Testament were written, many other pious stories and legends relating to Christ and His times were also widely circulated. As a result, in the early centuries of the Church, there was some confusion and doubt as to which books were inspired and biblical, and which were not. As far as is known, it was the Council of Hippo in A.D. 393 which first determined which books were inspired and were to be included in the Bible canon, a canon in every respect identical with the canon of the Council of Trent. Subsequent Councils confirmed this decision, and the Council of Trent, in 1546, formally canonized all the traditional books of the Bible. These books comprise the Old and the New Testaments, and it is a matter of faith for Catholics to believe that all passages of all books are equally inspired.

THE APOCRYPHA

Those books which were rejected by the Council of Hippo as being non-biblical belong to what is called the Apocrypha. These books treat largely of the incidents and events during the life of Christ not related in the books of the Bible. They are often well worth reading, as they offer much historical information not otherwise available. However, some of these stories have slightly heretical tendencies.

The Catholic use of the word ''Apocrypha,'' as defined above, should be distinguished from the incorrect Protestant use of the word. Protestants use this term to designate the seven books of the Bible included in the Catholic Bible canon, but not accepted or found in Protestant Bibles. These seven books are: Tobit, Judith, Wisdom, Sirach, Baruch, 1 and 2 Maccabees, and parts of Esther and Daniel. Protestants call the books found in the Catholic Apocrypha the Pseudepigraphal books.

HISTORY OF THE PROTESTANT CANON

The difference in the Catholic and Protestant Bibles arose in the following manner. The Jews living in the few centuries before Christ were divided into two groups — the Jews dwelling in Palestine and speaking Hebrew, and the large number of Jews scattered throughout the Roman Empire and speaking the Greek language, a consequence of the conquest of Alexander the Great of Greece.

CRITERIA OF THE JEWISH CANON

In the several centuries before the coming of Christ, the Jews in Palestine re-examined and eliminated some of the books from the existing collection as not in harmony with the Law of Moses and as of doubtful inspiration. The Pharisees set up four criteria which their sacred books had to pass in order to be included in the revised Jewish canon: (1) They had to be in harmony with the Pentateuch (Torah or Law); (2) They had to have been written before the time of Ezra; (3) They had to be written in Hebrew; (4) They had to have been written in Palestine.

BIBLE BOOKS ELIMINATED BY THE JEWS

The application of these arbitrary criteria eliminated Judith, probably written in Aramaic; Wisdom and 2 Maccabees, written in Greek; Tobit and parts of Daniel and Esther, written in Aramaic and probably outside of Palestine; Baruch, written outside of Palestine; and Sirach and 1 Maccabees, written after the time of Ezra. By the 1st Century after Christ, this revised canon was generally accepted by all Jews.

THE CHURCH RECOGNIZES THE ALEXANDRINE CANON

From the earliest times, the Christian Church recognized the Jewish canon of the Greek-Roman tradition, or Alexandrine canon, as being the true Bible. Jesus Himself quoted from this Bible, and not until the Reformation was this canon seriously challenged.

These seven disputed books are also called the deuterocanonical books, while the rest of the books of the Old Testament comprise the protocanonical books. By protocanonical books is meant the "books of the first canon," books of the Old Testament accepted by both Christians and Jews. The deuterocanonical books, "books of the second canon," are those seven books found only in the Catholic canon.

Luther rejected the deuterocanonical books of the Old Testament. At one time he also eliminated Hebrews, James, Jude, and the Apocalypse from the New Testament, but later Protestants reinserted them. Today the Catholic and Protestant New Testament books are identical.

LANGUAGES OF THE BIBLE

The books of the Bible were originally written in three languages: Hebrew, Aramaic, and Greek. Aramaic is a branch of the Semitic languages, and was the language used in Palestine in the time of Christ. It is the language Christ spoke. Hebrew is a Semitic language which originated in Canaan and which was passed on by Abraham and his descendants, reaching its greatest glory in the reigns of David and Solomon. It was the language of the Holy Land until about the 3rd

Century B.C., when it was supplanted by Aramaic. The Greek language as used in the Bible is not the classical Greek as we know it today, but a dialect spread throughout the known world of the time by conquests of Alexander the Great.

Most of the books of the Old Testament were written in Hebrew, while all of the New Testament, excepting Matthew, was written in Greek. The Book of Wisdom and 2 Maccabees were also written in Greek. Portions of the Book of Daniel, Ezra, Jeremiah, and Esther, and all of Tobit, Judith, and the Gospel of St. Matthew were written in Aramaic.

TEXTUAL DIVISION OF THE BIBLE

The Bible as originally set down was not divided into chapter and verse as we know it today. Stephen Langton, Archbishop of Canterbury in the 13th Century, first divided the Bible text into Chapters. Santes Pagninus divided the Old Testament chapters into verses in 1528, and Robert Etienne, a printer in Paris, did the same for the New Testament in 1551.

THE OLD TESTAMENT

In the past we have tended to think of the books of the Bible as historical (such as Genesis, Exodus, Kings, and Maccabees); legal (Leviticus, Deuteronomy, etc.); prophetic (predicting the future); and so on.

An appreciation of the Jewish method of dividing the books (given on the previous page) may be a more helpful method. The first five books of the Bible (Genesis, Exodus, Leviticus, Numbers and Deuteronomy) were considered the books central to their faith. They were called Torah in Hebrew. The word Torah means an "instruction" not just a lesson but the kind of instruction a parent gives to a child when he wants him to obey.

Many of the books which we think of as historical (Joshua, Judges, Samuel and Kings) were considered "prophetic" by the Jews. By prophetic they meant an inspired sermon. These books recounted events from their history in order to moralize. They were sermons from history. In these books we may find prophets appearing but they are prophets who act. They leave us no long sermons. They are part of the rough and tumble of life. Important Kings may hardly be mentioned simply because they offered few examples to be imitated. Unimportant kings may receive more attention because they were good men. This is not our modern way of writing history, of course. Even for them it was not primarily history. It was rather religious editorializing. We may err by thinking of them as history. They are that but they are much more. The Jews called them the "former" prophets not because they came earlier in time but because they were bound into the Bible first.

The Prophetical books, the "latter prophets," whether written by the prophet himself or by a disciple, are inspired sermons. A prophet is a man who speaks for God and to his own times. He is a man concerned about his own world. He sometimes predicts the future. More frequently it is the immediate future. When he does so he is exercising a power that is not, strictly speaking, prophetic. It is an additional power from God. We tend to be led astray if we think of them primarily as predictors of the future.

The "Writings" are a catch-all for other books. Chronicles, which we think of as history, is a many-faceted book. To call it history is to miss many of its qualities. The poetry of Psalms and Wisdom-literature such as Proverbs is also included in this section. Daniel, which is a special kind of literature known as "apocalyptic" is included here though in the past we thought of it as among the Prophetic books.

Those books accepted by the Septuagint or Greek version of the Hebrew Bible but which the Jews rejected after the time of Christ are called "Deutero-Canonical" books. They, together with parts of Daniel and Esther, are not accepted as part of the Bible by Protestants or Jews. Catholics have always revered them as such since the earliest days of the church.

THE NEW TESTAMENT

In the New Testament we think of the "four gospels" of Matthew, Mark, Luke and John. These are the Gospels (or "good news") of Jesus Christ. But Acts of Apostles is the same kind of book. It is the "gospel of the Holy Spirit" and depicts the work of Christ continued in the early Church.

Though none of the "four gospels" are a "Life of Christ" for they tell us very little about most of His life, they do use incidents from the life of Christ to illustrate His teaching. Primarily then, the Gospels and Acts (also written by Luke) present us with the message, mission, and works of Christ. Every man who saw Christ saw him from a unique perspective. These four men we call Evangelists saw him from their own particular points of view.

"Epistles" are letters of various kinds. Some are like "letters to the editor" that were intended to be widely circulated, not only in the church to which they were sent but throughout the territory. Others were quite private. Charming little "Philemon" is a short note of Paul to a convert. Still others were written in the style of a letter as a style of literature. The Epistles of James and Peter are really treatises on doctrine.

The last book of the Bible, "Revelations" (or Apocalypse) is the only New Testament book written in a very popular style of the day. As with Daniel and Ezekiel in the Old Testament it was written in a kind of code of persecuted members of God's people recounting God's saving acts in the past in the face of present trials. They look forward, also, to saving acts in the future based on their faith in Him.

INSPIRATION OF THE BIBLE

THE BOOKS of the Bible have as their principal author the Holy Spirit, although He Himself did not write them. The Holy Spirit inspired the human authors of the Bible to write down in their own words, and in the manner and style of the day, what He wanted them to write, and He guided them to the extent that they wrote faithfully what they had been taught. This working together of God and man in the writing of the Bible is called inspiration. This inspiration covers not only matters of faith and morals, but extends as well to the facts of history as related, and to the whole Bible.

BIBLICAL INSPIRATION DEFINED

Pope Leo XIII, in his encyclical *Providentissimus Deus,* explains how inspiration affected the biblical writers. "By supernatural power God so moved and impelled them to write. He was so present to them, that they first rightly understood, then willed faithfully to write down, and finally expressed in apt words and with infallible truth the things which He ordered, and those only."

BIBLICAL REFERENCES TO ITS INSPIRATION

Besides the infallible teaching of the Church as to the inspiration of the Bible, we have reliable historical evidence as well. Many indirect passages in the Old Testament refer to its inspiration (Isaiah 8, 1; Wisdom 7, 15), and in the New Testament St. Peter refers to it in 2 Peter 1, 20-21.

TRADITION CONFIRMS BIBLICAL INSPIRATION

Tradition, too, provides overwhelming proof that from the earliest days of the Church it was believed that the Bible was inspired. The Fathers of the Church allude to it in many passages, stating variously that the books were inspired, that God is the Author of the Bible, and that the sacred writers were the instruments of God. Throughout its history, the Church has made many official pronouncements in ecclesiastical documents reaffirming the fact of inspiration.

EXTENT OF INSPIRATION

The Council of Trent on April 8, 1546, decreed that "those entire books with all their parts as have been accustomed to be read in the Catholic Church" must be considered as sacred and canonical. This was reaffirmed by the Council of the Vatican in 1870. In the centuries since this decree, Catholic theologians differed on two points of interpretation, as to whether matters of faith and morals alone were to be considered inspired or to whether inspiration extended just to important matters. These questions were settled by Pope Leo XIII in his encyclical *Providentissimus Deus,* in which he reaffirmed the decisions of the Council of Trent and emphasized that the Bible in all its parts was inspired and that a stated fact must be accepted as falling under inspiration, down to the most insignificant item; that is, *the whole Bible is the Word of God.*

HISTORY OF THE BIBLE

No ORIGINAL MANUSCRIPTS of the Bible have come down to us, due to the perishable material upon which they were written and the fact that the Roman emperors decreed the destruction of the manuscripts during the Christian persecutions. While none of the original manuscripts are known to exist, some very ancient transcriptions have survived the years.

ANCIENT MANUSCRIPTS OF THE BIBLE

The oldest Hebrew manuscript known is a copy of the Book of Isaiah, written in Hebrew in the 2nd Century. It was found in 1947 in a cave near Jericho. The oldest Greek fragment known to exist is in the John Ryland Library in Manchester, England. This fragment is from the 2nd Century A.D. Several thousand other ancient Greek manuscripts have been found, the three most complete and important being the Codex Sinaiticus, Codex Vaticanus, and the Codex Alexandrinus, all probably of the 4th and 5th Century after Christ. The Codex Vaticanus is in the Vatican library.

EARLY TRANSLATIONS OF THE BIBLE

The most important early translations of the Bible were the Septuagint and the Vulgate. The Septuagint, a Greek translation of the Old Testament, was begun about 250 B.C. and completed about 100 B.C. This translation was made for the Jews of Egypt so that they could read their sacred books in Greek, the only language that most of them understood at that time. Before long, the Septuagint was widely used in Palestine and distributed throughout the Greek-speaking peoples of the Mediterranean world during the time of Christ and for the 1st Century or longer of the Christian era. The Apostles of Christ used this translation in their teaching.

THE BIBLE IN THE FIRST
TWO CENTURIES AFTER CHRIST

In the early days of the Church, the Scriptures were read at divine services in Greek. An early translation from Greek to Latin was needed for many of the Christians in the West could not understand Greek. Such translations, gathered together, made up the first Latin Bible. Prepared by so many different people of varying education, the translations were uneven and inaccurate. By the 2nd Century, there were a number of Latin translations, the most widely circulated being the *Old Latin,* or *Itala*.

ST. JEROME AND THE VULGATE TRANSLATION

Because of the numerous variant readings of the *Itala*, due to the copyists, revisers, or translators, Pope Damasus requested St. Jerome to revise and correct the New Testament. St. Jerome began his revision with the four Gospels and then revised the remaining books of the New Testament, but more hurriedly. The work was completed at Rome about A.D. 383-4. After the death of Pope Damasus, St. Jerome went to the Holy Land. He spent 34 years there, devoting his time to revising the Bible, to exegetical works, but mainly to the great work of his life — the translation of the protocanonical books of the Old Testament from Hebrew into Latin. This work extended over a period of fifteen years and it was a prodigious task, for the modern Vulgate is made up of: (a) the protocanonical books of the Old Testament, with the exception of the Psalter, translated from the Hebrew by St. Jerome; (b) the deuterocanonical books of Tobit and Judith from the Aramaic by St. Jerome; (c) the deuterocanonical books of Wisdom, Sirach, Baruch, and 1 and 2 Maccabees from the Old Latin unrevised by St. Jerome; (d) the deuterocanonical parts of Daniel from the Greek of Theodotion and of

Esther from the Septuagint; and (e) the New Testament revised from the Old Latin by St. Jerome.

THE VULGATE SUPERSEDES ALL OTHER VERSIONS

As St. Jerome's work on the Old Testament was a work of private enterprise, it met great opposition. He was accused of changing the text of the Bible, which was familiar to the people in the *Itala* or Old Latin. However, as time went on, the great merits of his work were recognized. By the 9th Century, Jerome's version was universally accepted. In view of its general adoption, it gradually assumed the name of "Vulgate," the "disseminated" or people's Bible.

THE CHURCH APPROVES THE VULGATE

On April 8, 1546, the Church, in the Council of Trent, designated the Vulgate as the official Church translation. To this day the Vulgate remains the official version of the Church, and translations of it are found in practically every language in the world. However, it does not mean that it is to be preferred over the Septuagint or over original manuscripts, or that it was entirely free from error. On the contrary, the Church recognized certain limitations in the translations from the beginning, and ordered a revision. This revised version was published in 1592 under Pope Clement VIII.

THE VULGATE FROM JEROME TO GUTENBERG

Jerome's text suffered many vicissitudes throughout the ages. In assembling a complete Bible, copyists would take some of their readings, by misadventure, from the old Latin texts and some from the Vulgate; both texts were in circulation. A monk might have memorized several passages from the old version in school, then, in writing a copy of the Vulgate, subconsciously lapse into the old phrasing so familiar to him. Some of the transcribers were not exercising a critical sense and would incorporate texts from other manuscripts, parallel passages, and texts from the liturgy.

The invention of printing only multiplied these problems for a time, but eventually scholars were able to print a text near to the text as it came from the hands of St. Jerome. While the Vulgate became the official version of the Western Church, it did not prevent other translations from being made. A Coptic version appeared in the 2nd Century; Ulfilas, an Arian bishop, made a Gothic translation in the 4th Century, and there were numerous Syrian, Armenian, Georgian, Arabic, and Slavonic versions in the early centuries.

GUTENBERG AND THE FIRST PRINTED BIBLE

The invention and development of a practical printing process by Gutenberg in the 15th Century did more to revolutionize and modernize the world than any other invention. Prior to this, all manuscripts and books had to be copied by hand and only the very wealthy could ever afford to have one. At once the tedious work of the professional copyist was ended. Not only did it do away with the copyist, it eliminated the many human errors made in copying.

By 1450 Gutenberg had developed the art of printing so well that he was ready to print his first book; the first book printed was the Bible, in the Latin Vulgate translation. About two years were spent in printing and binding the Bible, and it was completed in 1452. Over 200 copies were printed in the first edition.

THE BIBLE IN PRINT

With the invention of printing, the Bible ran through edition after edition — 124 in the first 50 years, all sponsored by the Catholic Church. By the time Luther's New Testament appeared in 1522 there were 14 complete editions in German. Parallel with this in time was the appearance of 11 Italian translations, 10 French, 2 Bohemian, one Flemish, and one Russian.

THE BIBLE IN ENGLISH

The first complete English translation of the Bible appeared relatively late, probably not until the 14th Century. However, the English people were not without the Bible in those early years, as the Latin Vulgate was widely disseminated and in daily use. In addition, numerous paraphrases, translations, and commentaries of various Bible stories were well known through scop and gleeman, the popular storytellers of their day.

EARLY HISTORY NOT DEFINITELY KNOWN

Much of the earlier history of the Bible in English still remains a mystery. Tradition holds that Aidan, Bishop of Landisfarne, who died in 651, encouraged his followers to read the Scriptures in their own tongue. Aldhelm, Bishop of Sherborne until his death in 709, is said to have translated the Psalms into the Saxon language. Between 721 and

901 various writers, including the Venerable Bede, Eadfrith, Alcuin, and King Alfred, are believed to have translated parts or all of the Bible stories into Old English. In the 10th Century, a translation of the first seven books of the Bible and the Book of Job made by Aelfric, Archbishop of Canterbury from 994 to 1005, was in circulation.

During the time between the death of Aelfric and the reputed work of Wyclif in 1380, other translations are reported to have existed. However, this was a period of great transition in the English language, and practically nothing remains of these writings. It was not until the 15th Century that English as we know it today emerged as a definite language.

WYCLIF'S TRANSLATION

The next important English version is the so-called Wyclif translation, of which over 150 manuscripts are extant. It is taken indirectly from the Vulgate. Much doubt has been cast recently on the theory that Wyclif was responsible for this pre-Reformation Bible in recent years, since the translation is largely Catholic in tone and diction and since most of the manuscripts of this version were found in the possession of notably Catholic families.

THE DOUAY-RHEIMS TRANSLATION.

The first complete and printed Catholic English translation that is definitely known appeared rather late, at the turn of the 16th Century. This is known as the Douay-Rheims version. It was a translation of the Latin Vulgate and was produced in France by English scholars who had fled the Catholic persecutions in England. The New Testament was published in Rheims in 1582 and the Old Testament in Douay in 1610.

Since the Douay-Rheims translation, the English language has undergone continuous changes. It was necessary, therefore, to revise and bring the Bible up to date from time to time. Bishop Challoner of England undertook and published a complete revision of the Douay-Rheims in 1750, and several less successful revisions appeared between that time and the 20th Century.

PROTESTANT BIBLICAL SCHOLARSHIP

Besides the Catholic versions of the Bible mentioned above, numerous Protestant versions of the Bible in English have appeared since the Reformation. William Tyndale (1484-1536) was one of the first Protestant translators of the Bible. His translation is especially noteworthy because he translated from the original Greek versions then available to him rather than from the traditional Vulgate.

Miles Coverdale translated and printed a complete English Bible in 1535. Coverdale's translation was the first English edition of the Bible to separate the deuterocanonical books from the protocanonical books. The deuterocanonical books were put in the back of the regular Bible text.

Between the publication of Coverdale's Bible and the King James or Authorized Version, other less important translations took place. Noteworthy among these were the Taverner's Bible, the Great Bible, Cranmer's Bible, the Geneva Bible, and the Bishop's Bible.

THE KING JAMES BIBLE

When James I ascended the throne of England in 1603, numerous and variant Protestant Bibles were in circulation. In 1604 preparations were, therefore, made to undertake a revision of the Protestant Bible. A group of scholars was organized, and using the Bishop's Bible as the basis for their new translation, produced the King James Version, which was published in 1611.

While of great literary merit, Protestants themselves recognized many serious defects in the translation. In 1881-1885 a revision was made, and this is popularly known as the Revised Version. Many other modern versions are also published today, the most important, perhaps, being the Revised Standard Version published in 1952. More recently the New English Version, among others have been published.

PRESENT CATHOLIC BIBLICAL SCHOLARSHIP

Pope Leo XIII gave the modern impetus to Bible study when he issued his famous encyclical, *Providentissimus Deus,* which set up standards for all future Bible scholarship. In addition, he established the Biblical Commission in 1902 to study and to give answers to biblical questions. In 1890 M. J. Lagrange, O. P., founded the Ecole Biblique at Jerusalem and also established the periodical, *Revue Biblique.* The Biblical Institute was established in Rome in 1908 by Pius X to give advanced training to biblical scholars.

In 1907 the Biblical Commission asked the Benedictine Order to undertake the task of revising the Vulgate, and this translation is still in process. Under the direction of the English Jesuit, Reverend Cuthbert Lattey, English and American scholars produced the Westminster edition of the Sacred Scriptures directly from the Greek and Hebrew texts. Other modern versions include a translation of the New Testament from the original languages by Fr. F. Spencer, O. P., and this was published in 1937. A complete translation of the Bible was made by Msgr. Ronald Knox of England in 1950 and has attained wide popularity because of the modernness and clarity of its language.

CONFRATERNITY TRANSLATION OF THE BIBLE

In the United States in the last 40 years, there has been a general revival of religion and the hierarchy felt a great need for an accurate modern translation of the Bible. Out of this has developed a new translation of the Bible by American Scripture scholars, sponsored by the Confraternity of Christian Doctrine.

The first task of this group was to prepare a modern edition of the Challoner revision of the Douay-Rheims English translation of the Bible. Proceeding with this, they published the New Testament in 1941, and then began the translation of the Old Testament. However, Pope Pius XII issued his Encyclical, *Divino Afflante Spiritu,* in 1943 which dealt with, among other things, the need for a new translation of the Bible directly from the original languages of the sacred authors. For this reason, the further revision of the Challoner-Douay-Rheims Version was abandoned.

The Confraternity then began the new translation of the Old Testament directly from the original Hebrew and of the New Testament from the original languages. The New American Bible is a culmination of their efforts.

REVISED NEW TESTAMENT TRANSLATION

Since the introduction of the New American Bible in 1970, interest and participation in Bible study has increased rapidly. Awareness of this trend combined with the experience of its actual use (especially in oral proclamation) provided a basis for a revision of the original New Testament text.

Begun in 1978 and completed in 1986, the threefold purpose of this revision (also expressed in the preface of the first edition) was: "to provide a version suitable for liturgical proclamation, for private reading and for purposes of study."

An additional concern of the editors was the production of a version as accurate and faithful to the original Greek text as possible. At the same time, special attention was paid to ensure that the language chosen not only reflected contemporary American usage, but eliminated all discrimination (especially against women) whenever possible.

More abundant introductions, footnotes and explanatory material were also added to facilitate devotional reading and make the revision more suitable for purposes of study.

The New American Bible is a Roman Catholic translation. This revision, however, like the first edition, is the result of collaboration with scholars from other Christian Churches, both among the revisors and members of the editorial board.

More abundant introductions, footnotes and explanatory material were also added to facilitate devotional reading and make the revision more suitable for purposes of study.

The New American Bible, like the First edition, is a Roman Catholic translation. This revision, however, is the result of collaboration with scholars from other Christian Churches, both among the revisors and members of the editorial board.

THE OLD TESTAMENT